Hope Discovered

By Gigi Sharpe Thornton

ISBN: 979-8519762830

ACKNOWLEDGEMENTS

First, I want to thank God for without Him none of this would have been possible.

Without these four people this little book of hope would not have been completed:

Firstly, I would like to thank my wonderful husband, Richard Thornton, who saw the potential in me to write my own devotionals.

Secondly, I would like to thank my Spiritual Coach Sister DeAnna Haynes who encouraged me to keep going.

Thirdly, not to forget my computer guy Lee Rodman.

Lastly, but not least, I want to thank my Minister Bryan Moten who helped me stay focused on what I was writing.

1 A HEART FOR GOD

And ye shall seek me, and find me, when ye shall search for me with all your heart. Jeremiah 29:13

Have there ever been times when you did not know what it was you were missing but you knew in your heart something was missing? I have spent a good part of my early adult life dealing with many types of addictions. I went from one addiction to another unfulfilled in what was missing yet mostly needed. As a child, my mom took us to church every Sunday and for every event the church had until I turned sixteen. At that point she said, "Now you have to decide if you're going to go to church or not. The choice is yours." I stop going. Young and dumb. I now realize that what she allowed me to do at that age was unwise. I started experimenting with various drugs and became a wild and uncontrollable teen. I got pregnant four times and had three beautiful children and yet I was still searching for something else.

When we left New York and moved to Hollywood, South Carolina I was very unhappy. I did the only thing I knew how to do, get high. That is when all the trouble began. I was in and out of jail, was raped (more than once), and hopelessly living in the street. I was lost but I would always ask God to please help me. I knew deep within my heart that He was the only one who could. I called on Him day and night no matter where I was or what I was doing. I remember thinking to myself God does not hear you. Look at all that you are doing. Why should He listen to you? Nevertheless, I continued to cry out to Him. Help me! That day He did. I ended up going to jail. That turned out to be the new beginning I so desperately needed. Who knew that this was how He saved me from myself. I read my Bible every day, sometimes all day. I went to every Bible study they would allow me to attend. I prayed for others and myself. I talked to God every chance I could. I learned about fasting and did that too. I needed for Him to take over and He did! After that last release from jail, I came home, went to church, and was baptized into Christ. Today I live for Christ. I told you this short story about part of my life to let you know that no matter how you feel or think about your situation or station in life, God loves you and He is waiting on you to call out to Him. Search for Him with your whole heart. He promised that you will find Him. (Read Matthew 7:8)

Prayer: Heavenly Father, thank you for hearing my cries. I know that right now you are listening to those who are calling out for you and you will save them. Thank you for the mercies you show me every day. In Jesus Name, Amen.

2 CURRENT CIRCUMSTANCES

"I waited patiently for the Lord; He turned to me and heard my "cry" Psalm 40:1

Many times, in life we will go through different trials and tribulations. How we deal with these trials and tribulations is key., While going through a particular situation we often to fix it on our own. As if we could! Why is it so easy to forget how far we have come and who bought us through.

Two years ago, my roommate and I experienced the fear of not being able to get a place to live on our own. My credit was way below where I thought it should be. My bank account was not where it should have been to move out on my own. With only a few weeks left before we had to move out, we both had to make some extremely hard decisions about where to go. Well, I went to take a CPR class one day and while there found out that Section 8 was taking applications online. To make a long story short I started that application but never got to finish it before I got locked out of that website. What I thought was another setback and disappointment was a blessing. A few days later I received a letter in the mail stating that my application was accepted for Section 8 low-cost housing. God had it already worked out. By the way I did pass the CPR class as well

Well today I am facing similar circumstances for purchasing a home. However, I am not reacting in quite the same manner. I have prayed and asked for guidance. I know that he will show me what I need to do and then sit back and let him do the rest.

In Hebrews 11 many had faith and trusted in God promises even though they did not live to see his promises come to fruition" There are many plans in a man's heart. Nevertheless, the Lord's counsel-that will stand. (Proverbs 19:21) Bottom line do not let your current circumstances direct the course of your life, trust Gods plan for your life. Read Proverbs 3: 5-6

Prayer: Dear Lord help me to remember that you knew the plans you have had for my life long before the world even was. Show me how to live one day at a time trusting you always. In Jesus Name, Amen.

3 FEAR OF THE UNKNOWN

God has not given us a spirit of fear, but of power, love and a sound mind, 2 Timothy 1:7

As children our imaginations would run wild, especially at night. Daddy, Daddy there is a monster under my bed. The streetlight outside the bedroom window casting strange images from the tree branches onto the walls. We pull the covers up over our heads as if that would stop those images from playing over and over in our minds. Fear is real.

As adults we often let our imaginations run wild too. When faced with the uncertainties of life fear steps right on in. There are so many different types of fears that the world calls phobias. These can be quite real to the person experiencing them. There is one named Xenophobia. Xenophobia is defined as the irrational sensation of fear experienced about a person or a group of persons as well as situations that are perceived as strange or foreign. It is the fear of anything that is beyond one's comfort zone Fear of the unknown! Fear is a negative emotion. Which can turn into negative thoughts then negative actions.

God wanted to bless the children of Israel in Numbers 13.

He told Moses to send them into a land flowing with milk and honey. Those twelve spies went and ten came back fearful of what they saw and considered to be giants in the land. However two of the twelve Joshua and Caleb (Numbers 14: 6-9) did not fear the inhabitants of the land because they trusted in God.

Satan is the author of fear and he will use it anyway he can. God tells us time and again that as Christians we have nothing to fear if we keep our focus on him. "You will keep him in perfect peace , whose mind is stayed on You" (Isaiah 26:3). There is a scripture that I go to besides 2 Timothy 1:7 and that is Colossians 3: 15 let the peace of God rule in your heart... When fear comes knocking on the door of your heart meditate on scriptures about peace that are all throughout His word. John 14:27, John 16:33, Philippians 4:13 and many more.

Prayer: Father God I sometimes become fearful about many things happening in my life and in this world. I want to trust you and believe in my heart that everything will be alright. Take hold of my heart and make it like yours. In Jesus Name, Amen.

4 FEELING ALL ALONE

Fear not, for I am with you; be not dismayed, for I am your God. I will strengthen you, Yes I will be with you. Isaiah 41:10

Have you ever been in a room full of people, or a family function surrounded by your loved ones but still felt alone or lonely?

Know this, you are not by yourself feeling this way. Countless others and those in biblical days felt this way. While David was on the run from Saul (1 Sam) he felt alone. There were occasions when even Jesus experienced loneliness. Once while in the Garden of Gethsemane. He went to pray before He was to be crucified. And while He was on the cross the Father left him all alone. In both instances there were people around and near Him. Yet He still felt alone.

When you feel that you have no one to talk to. No one to tell that your heart is hurting or even when you are anxious about a matter. Remember God, Jesus and the Holy Spirit are always with you. Pour out your heart, be honest about what you are feeling. He knows anyway what is in your heart. Jesus felt all the things we today feel. He experienced anguish, pain, sadness and much more. All the things we have felt at one time or another. I know it can be hard sometimes to remember that he is with you, but he is and always will be. He promised that He would never leave you nor forsake you. (Deuteronomy 31:6) He will listen and the best part of it is that he will have compassion for you. He will not leave you in the state that you are in. Get on your knees and pray. Get up and praise Him about what you are feeling, and it will all melt away. Weeping may endure for a night, but JOY comes in the morning. (Psalms 30:5)

Know that God is omnipresent and omniscient. He is everywhere and knows all things. That means he sees you and knows what you are feeling. He is made over 5000 promises in his word. In those promises he says he will never leave you nor forsake you (Hebrews 13:5). Believe him he will not lie. Now remember this as well. He said," cast all your cares on him for he careth for you. (1 Peter 5:7) That word careth means he continues to care for you forever. That is good news all by itself.

Prayer: Heavenly Father when I start to have feelings of loneliness help me to remember you have promised to be with me always. In Jesus Name, Amen.

5 FREE WILL

This day I call the heavens and the earth as witnesses against you that I have set before your life and death, blessings, and curses. Now I call on heaven and earth to witness the choice you make. Oh, that you would choose life, so that you and your descendants might live! You can make this choice by loving the Lord your God, obeying him, and committing yourself firmly to him. This is the key to your life. And if you love and obey the Lord, you will live long in the land the Lord swore to give your ancestors Abraham, Isaac, and Jacob.'(Deuteronomy 30:19-20)

Growing up I remember my mother taking us to church twice on Sundays and during the week for Bible Study. At this Baptist church they seem to have always had more things going on than there were days in the week. Nevertheless, my mom had us there whenever the doors were opened. Whether we wanted to go or not. She would always say" As long as you're living in my house when I go you go!' At the age of sixteen we were given privilege of choice in deciding if we wanted to attend church or not. I never understood that but when I turned sixteen, I made the choice not to go any more. Shortly after that I started using drugs and ditching school to go to parties. This type of living lasted more than twenty years. A lot has happened over that period in my life. Too much to write about here.

God does the same thing he offers us free will. He gives us the ability to make choices in our lives. We have the choice to do right or wrong, good, or evil, to live for him or not. He wants a relationship with us, but he will not force himself into our lives. He gives us the choice to choose life with Him or without Him. I must tell you though that life with the Lord is so much easier. I struggled for a long time before I came to the Lord some ten years ago. I made a conscious choice to turn my life over to the Lord. I was sick and tired of being sick and tired. My life was an endless cycle of drugs, heartache, and pain but God knew from the beginning that I would seek him with my whole heart. Even before He made the world, God loved us and chose us in Christ to be holy and without fault in his eyes (Ephesians 1:4)

I still struggle from time to time in this life, but I do not have to struggle alone any more I have Chris! Decide today to live for Christ. Life is far better.

Prayer: Lord God It is so good to know that you knew me long before I even was. Help those who do not know you to make the choice to come to you before it is too late. Thank you for longsuffering on behalf of all. In Jesus Name, Amen.

6 GIANTS IN MY LIFE

David said to the Philistine," you come against me with sword and spear and javelin. But I come against you in the name of the Lord Almighty, the God of the armies of Israel whom you have divided. This day the Lord will hand you over to me, and I will strike you down and cut off your head. Today I will give the carcasses of the Philistine army to the birds of the air and the beast of the earth, and the whole world will know that there is a God in Israel. All those gathered here will know that it is not by sword or spear that the Lord saves; for the battle is the Lord's, and he will give all of you into our hands." 1 Samuel 17: 45-47

Have you ever felt like the things going on in your life were too much for you to deal with? Your problems seemed so huge that you felt like throwing in the towel? Hold on to the towel! God is bigger than any problem or issue you may be dealing with. I have heard this quote "stop telling God how big your problem is but tell your problem how big your God is." We tend to buckle under too much pressure. Especially when we are trying to handle the problems on our own. Specifically, the ones we have no control over!

In the story about David and Goliath, King Saul wanted to

flee from the giant in his life. I guess he forgot who was the strongest, namely God. He cowered at the mere thought of having to go up against this giant of the Philistines and quite possibly dying by his hands. You and I today do not have to worry about the giants in our lives or at least what we perceive to be giants in our lives. God has given us the power as Christians to fight. Not only that, but He has also promised through his word that He will always be with us. Remember in most cases the battle is not yours but the Lords.

Prayer: Forgive me for cowering in the face of adversity. Father, please increase my faith in you and help me to stand on your word. You have promised that You will fight for me. Help me to put all my trust in you. I give all my burdens to you because your yoke is easy, and your burdens are light. In Jesus name, Amen.

7 HOPE AT THE END OF THE ROPE

If I shut the sky so that there is no rain, or if I command the locust to devour the land, if I send pestilence among my people, if my people who are called by my name will humble themselves, pray, seek my face, and turn from their wicked ways, then I will hear from heaven, will forgive their sin, and will heal their land. 2 Chronicles 7:13-14

Never in my life have I experienced a year like this one. We are dealing with a pandemic of epic proportions. We call it the Corona Virus dubbed Covid-19. This disease has killed over two hundred and fifty thousand people already and more are dying every day. So many more have contracted this virus and are in their homes quarantining themselves. Then we have those who know this virus is deadly and running wild but seem not to care and are living their lives haphazardly thinking that it could not affect them. It has taken over our world and this nation in which we live. It has affected people's livelihood, the government and so much more. There were many other diseases that were deadly before this one such as smallpox, yellow fever, the Spanish flu and many others strains of the flu that killed thousands of people. Somehow scientists always come up with a cure.

In the Old Testament God sent ten plagues on Egypt so that Pharaoh would let the Israelites go. Then there was the time when the people of Israel spoke against God, and He sent fiery serpents upon the people and many of them died after being bitten. However, after confessing their sins against God, God gave Moses' instructions on how they would be saved from death (read Numbers 21:6-9). As before, all God wants is for us to come back to Him and He in turn will heal our land. He loves us and wants the best for us. He is also a just God and when we go astray, He brings us back by any means necessary. So, there is hope for our nation and this world in which we live.

Prayer: Lord God forgive us of our sins and give us new hearts to follow You. Heal our land just as You have done in times past. We repent with our whole hearts of our wickedness. Thank you for the love you have shown us in the death, burial, and resurrection of your son Jesus Christ. In Jesus' name we pray, Amen.

8 IN HIS STRENGTH

"My grace is sufficient for you, for My strength is made perfect in weakness." {2 Corinthians 12:9}

I have been dealing with various illnesses and pain for over ten years now. The doctors have given me medications for this and that which help short term. I am sitting at my computer right now dealing with pain in my feet that makes me want to cry. When a person is dealing with pain, they tend to say things like, why me? I do it sometimes and then I remember who I serve and how powerful He is. I was praying and as I was asking God to heal me and take the pain away. While praying the Holy Spirit reminded me that somewhere somebody does not have feet

Pain is a reminder and motivator to pray. It will keep you humble. I really love this passage of scripture. It has always given me hope in Jesus' and in the mighty power. I am not sure what the Apostle Paul's thorn in the flesh was. According to the scripture he was given this thorn in the flesh by a messenger of Satan to buffeted (beat, torment) him. (2 Corinthians 12:7) He, too, like most of us asked God to remove the thorn (pain) from his body. God knows better than we do if He answered all our prayers according to our own desires then we will forget Him as our deliverer and glory would fall upon ourselves instead of Him.

He made us to be strong, but we must not forget where our strength comes from!

Prayer: Father God Almighty I thank you for reminding me where my strength comes from. I humble myself before you and lift your mighty name in praise through my weaknesses. You are my refuge and strength. In Jesus Name, Amen.

9 INSTRUCTION MANUALS

Grace and peace be multiplied to you in the knowledge of God and of Jesus our Lord, as His divine power has given to us all things that pertain to life and godliness, through the knowledge of Him who called us by glory and virtue. 2 Peter 1-3

When we purchase certain items for our homes, they come with an instruction manual or booklet telling us step by step how to assemble that item. How often do we open the box, toss the manual aside and start putting that item together? Honestly. most of the time. I too am guilty of doing this. Most of the time I find the instructions to be too difficult or just too tedious so I at the diagrams and try to assemble it. With this process it almost always never works out right. Recently, I bought a new television and without reading the instructions I proceeded to turn it on and set it up. Not only did I do that but hooked up other devices to the television as well. After doing so I could no longer get my cable channels. Why you ask? Yes, I asked myself the same thing. I never opened the booklet, but I called the cable company complaining because it did not work. They said" that particular television does not support their cable service." Had I just taken the time to read the booklet there was a chance all would have turned out fine.

We live our lives the same way when we do not take the time to read the Bible. We struggle with many things that happen in our lives and do not know why. From Genesis to Revelation, we can learn how to live. God gives us all we need in his word. Read Romans 13:13; Ephesians 5:8 and Matthew 5:16. Living our lives according to the word of God does not mean there will not be struggles but that He will always be with us and that we should aim to please and glorify Him by striving to continuously walk in His ways.

Prayer: Lord, thank you for your word that tells me how to live so that I may see you in heaven one day. Let it be a lamp unto my feet and a light unto my path. In Jesus Name, Amen.

10 LIFE HAPPENS

To everything there is a season, A time for every purpose under heaven. Ecclesiastes 3:1

In this life we will experience trials, disappointments, setbacks, crushed dreams and much more. I know this young woman who was a caregiver for my church sister and neighbor. Well things were happening in her life as we like to say, "back-to-back." It seemed to her that her life was spiraling out of control. She would come over and just to talk and cry. I suggested that we prayed every time, and we did. I am not sure if she believed that when we prayed that God was listening, but I believed. I knew from past experiences that God was listening and already working on her behalf before the prayer was even finished.

Trust and believe that life will throw you some curveballs. But it depends on how you chose to deal with those curveballs. As Christians, we should deal with life much differently than those who are in the world. Not just to help other Christians get through their trials but also so that others can put their hope in Christ. Paul states this about God "the God of all comfort" , who comforts us in our troubles " that we may be able to comfort those who are in any trouble, with the comfort with which we ourselves are comforted by God"(2 Corinthians 1:3-4). Sometimes the troubles we go through in life are not for us but so that God can show us how to comfort others through their troubles.

Prayer: Dear God, thank you for comforting me through the troubles, trials, and tribulations that life throws my way so that I may in turn give that comfort to others. Lord God show me who needs to be comforted today by your spirit. In Jesus Name, Amen.

11 LONG DISTANCE RACE

Do you not know that those who run in a race all run but one receives the prize? Run in such a way that you may obtain it.
1 Corinthians 9:24

Every year here in Charleston, South Carolina there is an event called The Cooper River Bridge Run. People from all around the world come for this event. There are those who compete for a cash prize, some for sport and some just to be out there. I reckon those who compete for the prize, are the ones who train the hardest. They know that you cannot just go and run and expect to win without training. I am not sure what that training may be like, but I would dare to say that there is plenty of stretching, walking, short sprints, eating right and let's not forget the muscle cramps. My point here is that they do not just get out there one day and say they are running to win a race. They put a lot of effort into winning.

As Christians we must run our Christian race to receive the incorruptible crown and eternal life with the Father. Running this race takes faith along with prayer, worship, and reading our Bible every day. No one thing will help us win the race but a combination of things. However, we cannot do any of these things on our own. The Father helps through the guidance of the Holy Spirit.

When I first became a baptized believer, I wanted so much to be like the "seasoned saints". I soon realized that their race was not my race and vice versa. I then began to learn what God wanted from me but at a pace that was different from all the other saints. After drinking spiritual milk, I later moved on to eating the meat of God's word. As I run this Christian, I ask God to strengthen me (Philippians 4:13). as I run. It is not always easy but with God all things are possible (Matthew 19:26).

Prayer: Father I thank you for accepting into your kingdom. I thank you for giving me all I need to run this race. Lord God, I thank you for your word which directs my steps each day you allow me to run. I look forward to running to see what the end is going to be for me. I want a mansion, robe, and a crown. In Jesus Name, Amen.

12 MAKE ME USABLE

Then I heard the voice of the Lord saying "Whom shall I send? And who will go for us?" And I said," Here am I . Send me!" Isaiah 6:8

Long before I became a Christian, I was a bona fide drug addict. I used to live and lived to use. Even then I was the type of person who would help someone anyway I could. Even if it were just to invite over for a meal, a place to sleep or just someone to talk to you. Although I was in bad shape, I wanted to help others. In Bible history God made a lot of saints usable. To name a few, Paul who was formerly Saul, and countless others. He even used Rahab the harlot.

Paul formerly Saul was persecuting the Church, followers of Jesus." As for Saul, he made havoc of the church, entering every house, and dragging off men and women, committing them to prison". Acts 8:3.

Saul on his way to Damascus had his first encounter with Jesus." Then Saul, still breathing threats and murder against the disciples of the Lord, went to the high priest and asked letters from him to the synagogues of Damascus, so that if he found any who were of the Way, whether men or women he might bring them bound to Jerusalem. As he journeyed, he came near Damascus, and suddenly a light shore around him from heaven. Then he fell to the ground, and heard a voice saying to him, "Saul, Saul, why are you persecuting Me?" And he said," Who are You, Lord? "Then the Lord said, "I am Jesus, whom you are persecuting. It is hard for you to kick against the goads. "So, he trembling and astonished, said, "Lord, what do You want me to do? "Acts 9:1-6 Paraphrasing, he went and not long after he was made usable for the Lord.

What God did with Paul He can today do for you and I. Drug free eleven years; God still uses my experience to help others. He cleaned me up and sent me out. Here I am! Send me!

Prayer: Dear Lord thank you for using me for your glory. Thank you for taking me from the streets into your kingdom. Help me to stay humble that you will continue to use me in a way that uplifts and encourages others and that you alone are glorified. In Jesus Name, Amen!

13 PERFECT IMPERFECTIONS

I will praise You, for I am fearfully and wonderfully made.
Psalms 139:14

When I was a teenager, I hated my body. In junior high
school my body shape was straight up and down, a stick I used
to say. It bothered me that most of the girls had breast and
well, shapely bodies. I wondered why I had to be the odd one.
Middle age did not make me happy either. I am too round in
the middle. Yes, I know I should eat right if I do not want to
be overweight. Nevertheless, here I am wanting to be slender
again. How ironic is that! Why is it that I am never happy with
my appearance? I know there are many others out there that
feel the way I do about their bodies or there would be no
plastic surgeons. So many women face lifts, tummy tucks and
breast implants. Why? Men are not excluded; they spend hours
at the gym everyday working out. The older ones are probably
waiting to see that six pack appear again and others just to stay
fit. Either way, why do we try and fix how God made us?

God created us in his own image (Genesis 1:26) When we
were in our mother's womb God designed our bodies and our
looks. Some of us were born with a head full of hair and others

not so much. Some with fair skin and others with darker skin tone. The genes or DNA of our parents plays a big part in how we look too. But remember who created them. God makes no mistakes; we are all different in one way or another. Our gene sequences are different. No matter about all of that really because His spirit lives in each one of us. Our flesh just covers the spirit.

How wonderful is that? You are perfect just the way you are!

Prayer: Heavenly Father how wonderful are thy works. You created the whole world, and it is beautiful, then you created me and I am beautiful for I was made in your image. I lift up my hands in praise to you. You gave each member of my body a purpose and they all work together according to how you created me. Thank you. In Jesus Name, Amen.

14 SECRET SINS

You spread out our sins before you- our secret sins- and you see them all (Psalms 90:8(NLT)

The above scripture mentions our secret sins. We sin every day because it is in our nature. However, there is that one sin we think nobody knows about it but you. Have you heard that saying, "what you do in the dark will eventually come to the light?" It is true! Even if nobody sees you in that sin. God Sees Everything! You cannot hide anything from him. What is in your heart he knows. He knew before you were even born just what you would do and not do. In the very beginning of the Bible is the story about Adam and Eve. (Read Genesis 3) This is when sin came into the world.

God has given us commandments today as he did in times past. Those commandments are there to help us not to fall for the deceptions that Satan will place in our hearts. The natural man is weak. The good news is that our spirit man is strong. We must feed the spirit and not the flesh of the natural man. "Walk in the Spirit, and you shall not fulfill the lust of the flesh. For the flesh lusts against the Spirit, and the Spirit against the flesh; and these are contrary to one another, so that you do not do the things that you wish." (Galatians 5:16-17)

There is this saying I have heard before and you probably have heard it too. Goes like this: "Sin will take you farther than you had planned on going, keep you longer than you had planned on staying and cost you more than you had planned on paying." Paul said it best "For what I am doing I do not understand. For what I will to do, that I do not practice, but what I hate, that I do. If then, I do what I will not to do, I agree with the law that it is good. But now, it is no longer I that do it but sin that dwells in me For I know that in me (that is in my flesh) nothing good dwell; for to will is present with me, but how to perform what is good I do not find. For the good that I will do, I do not do; but the evil I will not do, that I practice. Now if I do what I will not to do, it is no longer I who do i, but sin that dwells in me." (Romans 7:15-20) So, see sin is a =m ugly monster that lives in all of us but there is hope. Jesus died for our sins once and for all. All we need to do is confess our sins and he will forgive us. The blood of Jesus cleanses us and His mercies are new every day. Keep fighting!

Prayer: Lord God thank you for your new mercies every day. Thank you for loving us so much that you sent Jesus to help us out of our sin problem. Thank you, Jesus, for being obedient to the Father so that we may be forgiven. In Jesus Name, Amen.

15 SPOKEN WORDS

Death and life are in the power of the tongue; and they that love it shall eat the fruit thereof. (Proverbs 18:21 KJV)

Words are powerful but they are empty until someone opens their mouth and speaks them. Have you ever thought to yourself at the end of the day, how many words you have spoken? Was there any true meaning to them? Were they positive or negative words? It is sad but most of the time we do not think before we speak and once the words are said we cannot take them back. People tend to just say whatever is on their mind. Which is okay if your thoughts are good. We can lift, encourage, praise and make others feel good with our words or just the opposite with putting one down with slander and hateful words.

In the book of James, third chapter, he has quite a bit to say about the tongue. Paraphrasing, our tongue can cause good or bad things to happen. Now and in the hereafter, for example, when I am sick, I speak healing scriptures over myself and begin to feel better. There were also times when I doubted that I could do something and would speak negatively saying "this is too hard, and I cannot do it."

Consequently, it does not get done. I am already defeated because I have already said it!

God will not only judge us on our actions(deeds) according to his word but also by every word we have spoken. "But I say to you that for every idle word man may speak, they will give an account of it in the day of judgement. For by your words, you will be justified, and by your words you will be condemned." Matthew 12:36-37

Prayer: Lord God help us keep our words pure and clean. May they always lift and encourage not only others but ourselves as well. May all that we say be for your glory. In Jesus Name, Amen.

16 STORMS OF LIFE

When the south wind blew softly, supposing that they had obtained their purpose, they weighed anchor and sailed along to Crete, close to shore. But before long, stormy winds beat down from shore, which is called Euroclydon. When the ship was caught and could not face the wind, we gave way to it and were driven along. (Acts 27:13-15)

A euroclydon is a cyclonic tempestuous northeast wind which blows in the Mediterranean mostly in autumn and winter. Euroclydon is not to be confused with the term Northeaster which is a separate storm system that forms in the northeastern part of the United States. Nonetheless, both are bad storms. Paul was falsely accused by the Jewish leaders, jailed, and transported by Roman soldiers on a ship headed to Rome to be tried by the Roman courts. On his way, the storm came and caused the ship he was on to be driven by God to the island of Malta. This was no mistake that the storm came at that precise time. This happened so that the people of Malta could believe in God through Paul's ability to heal the sick on the island.

Many storms will come and go in our lives. God knows all about them. It may be a serious illness, loss of a job, or bills that are due with the lack of money to pay them. Perhaps a family member or a friend's addiction is deeply affecting your life. Storms in our lives can come in many forms but how we choose to deal with them is essential to how they are resolved. God allows storms in our lives to test our faith and to nudge us to put our full trust and confidence in him. He will not only test us, but He will bring us through the storms in such a way that He alone receives the glory. Hang in there! Storms do not last always.

Prayer: Father God, help me to see you and trust you when the storms of life come my way. Strengthen me in my spirit (the inner man). All power comes from above and I am counting on you to see me through. In Jesus' name, Amen.

17 TEMPTATIONS

There hath no temptation taken you, but such as is common to man: but God is faithful, who will not suffer you to be tempted above that ye are able. 1 Corinthians 10:13

Have you ever been on a diet where you could not eat anything with sugar in it? No dairy? No meat? Well, I have, and it is called the Daniel Fast. A few of our church members do this at the beginning of every year since I believe the last five years or more. My daughter's birthday happens to fall on the thirty-first of January, and we always make plans to go out and eat. One would think after so many days that it would not bother me to watch them eating sumptuously but it did. I was tempted to just skip the fast for that meal. Then I remembered why I was doing the fast. It was not about pleasing my appetite but pleasing God.

Jesus himself was tempted after fasting forty days and forty nights in more ways than one was, he tempted However he did not give in. "Then Jesus was led by the Spirit into the wilderness to be tempted by the devil. After fasting forty days and forty nights he was hungry. The tempter came to him and said "If you are the Son of God tell these stones to become bread. Jesus answered, "It is written Man shall not live on bread alone, but on every word that comes from the mouth of God. "Then the devil took him to the holy city and had him stand on the highest point of the temple, "If you are the Son of God,' he said," throw yourself down. For it is written: "He will command his angels concerning you, and they will lift you up in their hands, so that you will not strike your foot against a stone. Jesus answered him "It is also written "do not put the Lord your God to the test." Again, the devil took him to an extremely high mountain and showed him all the kingdoms of the world and their splendor. "All this I will give you,' he said," If you will bow down and worship me.'Jesus said to him "Away from me Satan. For it is written,' Worship the Lord God and serve him only. "Then the devil left him, and angels came and attended him. (Matthew 4: 1-11)

Many times, in life we will be tempted in one way or another to do things we know in our hearts that we ought not to do. Temptations are not from God. When tempted no one should say "God is tempting me." For God cannot be tempted by evil, nor does he tempt anyone. (James 1:13)

Our temptations come from the lustful desires of our hearts. [Read 1John 2:16] Lust can be described like this: an intense longing, to have a strong desire for something. Remember when you are tempted that God promises to deliver you from that temptation when you look to him for help.

Prayer: Heavenly Father, there are so many temptations in this world. Things that are vying for my heart. Thank you, Father, for renewing my spirit day by day. Thank you for the many promises in your word to help me when temptation comes my way. In Jesus Name, Amen.

18 THE ENEMY WITHIN

The thief does not come except to steal, and to kill, and to destroy. I have come that they may have life, and that they may have it more abundantly. John 10:10

If you do not know it yet, there is a spiritual battle going on for your soul and your mind. The enemy is very crafty and slicker than oil on a rainy road. Have you ever just been thinking about some good thing and suddenly you start imagining how something bad can happen? It happens to me more than I care for it to. That my friend, is the enemy who we call Satan. He will plant seeds of doubt, unworthiness, and unspeakable things in your mind. Unfortunately, when this happens, we become our own worst enemy.

The thoughts we have tend to become our actions. So, it is important that we watch what we think about most. Scripture tells us this... "Finally, my brethren, whatever things are true, whatever things are noble, whatever things are just, whatever things are pure, whatever things are lovely, whatever things are of good report, if there is any virtue and if there is anything praiseworthy, meditate on these things." Philippians 4:8

Not trying to give him any credit, but even the word tells us that Satan was craftier than any other beasts God had made (Genesis 3:1). He uses all sorts of deceitful tricks on us, and it starts with the mind. It is hard sometimes to see him coming. He will use your family, friends, neighbors, co-workers, and even total strangers against you. He will use situations that occur in your life to make you doubt that God is even watching over you. To wreak havoc in your life is his job... plain and simple! There is hope found in God's word which says, "Finally my brethren, be strong in the Lord and in the power of his might. Put on the full armor of God, that you may be able to stand against the wiles of the devil." (Ephesians 6:10-11) The armor consists of the breastplate of righteousness, your feet shod with the preparation of the gospel of peace, the shield of faith, the helmet of salvation, the sword of the Spirit which is the word of God and do not forget to pray. This is paraphrased but you can find it all in Ephesians 6:10-18.

We cannot fight this type of fight in the flesh but in the spirit. "For we do not wrestle against the flesh and blood, but the rulers of the darkness of this age, against spiritual hosts of wickedness in the heavenly places (Ephesians 6:12). So, see the battle is in the heavenly places and the Lord has his angels fighting now. All we must do is get in that fight with the power that has been given to us.

Prayer: Heavenly Father thank you for giving me what I need to fight the enemy when he comes. Help me not to forget who I belong to and that I have power from on high. In Jesus' name, Amen.

19 THE MIND OF CHRIST

Let this mind be in you which was also in Christ Jesus.
Philippians 2: 5

The human brain weighs about 3.3 pounds and makes up
about two percent of a human body weight. Some people
believe that we only use ten percent of our brain, but a
neurologist Barry Gordon explained that most of the brain is
almost always active. I tend to believe that because my brain
is active from the time I wake up until I go to sleep, everyday!
Even when I am asleep and dreaming, I have no doubt my
brain is still working. I may not understand how it all works
but I do know that while it is working the things you think
about should be positive.

To have the mind of Christ we must think as He did. His
focus was always on pleasing the Father. Even to the point of
death. Jesus was meek and humble of heart(mind). Matthew
11:29 He said in his word " take my yoke upon you and learn
from me, for I am gentle and lowly in heart, and you will find
rest for your souls". Jesus only ever thought about others

above himself. He has a heart for the lost, the sick, the deaf and the blind. When He came down from heaven to save us it was the most selfless act ever.

To have a mind like Christ we must first be saved by faith in Christ. Then to think more like Him. hang be done through selfish ambition or conceit, but in lowliness of mind let each esteem others better than himself. Let each of you look out not only for his own interests, but also for the interests of others (Philippians 2: 3-4) His thoughts were always about what God wanted for us. Seeking and saving the lost. (Luke 19:10) Having compassion on those who needed compassion (Philippians 2:5). We must listen to the Holy Spirit that lives in us because he is Christ and knows the things of God. (John 16: 14)

Prayer: Lord God I want to be more like Christ. I want to think more like Christ. Fill me to overflowing with your spirit that my thoughts line up with Christ. In Jesus Name, Amen.

20 VAIN IMAGINATIONS

Casting down imaginations and every high thing that exalts itself against the knowledge of God and bringing into captivity every thought to the obedience of Christ. (2 Corinthians 10:5)

Webster describes the word **vain** like this too proud of your own appearance or achievements. Having no real value. Marked by futility or ineffectiveness. The meaning of imagination is the ability to imagine things that are not real: the ability to form a picture in your mind of something that you have not seen or experienced. There is nothing wrong with a healthy imagination but when we start to think too highly of ourselves 'God is not pleased. Romans 12:3 says:" For I say through the grace given to me, to everyone who is among you, not to think of himself more highly than he ought to think, but to think soberly as God has dealt to each one a measure of faith'.

Many times, in life we think we have accomplished things on our own forgetting that God has mapped out our lives long before we ever were. We can do nothing of ourselves. God gave us the abilities that we have or that we have learned. So, you just got that big promotion on the job and it came with lots of benefits and perks but now, with your head held high, you look down on the janitor who cleans toilets for less pay and benefits and think you're better. You think to yourself I could never clean toilets for a living.

Whatever we do in life should always be for the glory of God. No matter if it is working in a cushy office or cleaning toilets. Never think so highly of yourself that you forget who your creator is and how He gives you all you need. Romans 1:21 states "because, although they knew God, they did not glorify Him as God, nor were thankful, but became futile in their thoughts, and their foolish hearts were darkened."

Prayer: Lord, I never want to think too highly of myself. Humble my heart for your glory. In Jesus name, Amen.

21 WATCH AND PRAY

Watch and pray that ye enter not into temptation: the spirit indeed is willing, but the flesh is weak. Matthew 26:41

In this life we must always be on guard because the enemy which is Satan is alive and working against us. Watching spiritually means to be on the lookout for the snares and tricks of our enemy Satan. "Be sober, be vigilant, because your adversary the devil, as a roaring lion walketh about seeking whom he may devour." (1 Peter 5:8 KJV) In this world we are going to be tempted daily. How we choose to deal with that temptation is key. "No temptation has overtaken you except as is common to man; but God is faithful, who will not allow you to be tempted beyond what you are able, but with the temptation will also take a way of escape, that you may be able to bear it." 1 Corinthians 10:13

I was a bona fide drug addict for over twenty years. In those twenty years I did so many unthinkable things not only to myself but to others as well. Sin dominated over my life. Just before my fiftieth birthday I asked and begged God to let me die if I had to continue in that lifestyle. I did not want to keep doing the things I was doing. Nor did I care to live the way I was living any longer. God heard my cries for help, and he turned my life around just before I turned fifty. A friend directed me to the Church of Christ, and I was so moved by the word that was being preached I accepted the call. I was baptized that day. I have said that to say this - Although I gave my life to Christ back then, I still struggle in the flesh with that same addiction. I just choose not to use any more. Temptation comes in many different forms that could easily trip me up. The difference from then and now is that I have the power of prayer. One of the many gifts that God has given to me. I must always be on guard for the enemy and so should you.

Prayer: First I want to thank you Father for the gift of prayer. Had you not sacrificed your only begotten Son Jesus Christ I would never have been able to come boldly before the throne. Thank you for the Holy Spirit that lives inside of me guiding and leading me every day. Help me dear God to listen when You speak. Keep me from stumbling back but help me to stay on the path that leads to glory. Let thy will be done. In Jesus name, Amen.

22 WHAT ARE YOU THINKING ABOUT

Finally, brethren, whatever things are true, whatever things are just, whatever things are pure, whatever things are lovely, whatever things are of good report, if there is any virtue and if there is anything praiseworthy-meditate on these things. Philippians 4:8

Some days my thinking can be all screwy. I never can seem to focus on one thing at a time. Even then my thoughts are not always good. Out of nowhere I would think about bad things that could happen. Not only to me but other people as well. I think it is the weirdest thing. For example, when I think about all the mass shootings that have happened in 2019. I think about how to punish the shooters. My thoughts are gruesome and uglier than the act they have committed. That ought not be because as a Christian I should have the mind of Christ. (Philippians 2:5) Instead, my thoughts should be on what to say when I pray for those people.

Joyce Meyers wrote a book titled "The Battlefield of The Mind." Basically, she is letting us know that there is a war going on for our minds and in our minds. This war is real! Satan cannot read our minds, but he most certainly can influence us with external temptations. James 1:14 essentially states that we are drawn away by our own sinful nature and Satan uses that to his advantage We can easily be influenced by the things we see, read, and hear. Most certainly in these days and times television and radio can play a big part in what we think about. Seeing how they are mostly geared towards the world. Be careful of what you watch and listen to. Feed the spirit and not the flesh.

"I say then: walk in the Spirit, and you shall not fulfill the lust (sinful desires) of the flesh. For the flesh lusts against the Spirit, and the Spirit against the flesh; and these are contrary to one another, so that you do not do the things that you wish, but if you are led by the Spirit, you are not under the law...If we live in the Spirit, let us also walk in the Spirit. (Galatians5:13-18,25

Prayer: Heavenly Father help us to walk in the Spirit as we ought to. Give us a clean heart and renew a right spirit within us not desiring the things of this world but eternal things in heaven, guide us dear Lord. In Jesus Name, Amen.

23 WORST OF SINNERS

This is a faithful saying and worthy of all acceptance, that Christ Jesus came into this world to save sinners, of whom I am chief. 1 Timothy 1:15

In this passage of scripture Paul considered himself chief of sinners because of his unbelief in Jesus being the Messiah, the Savior of the world. He even went so far as to beating killing and imprisoning and killing many believers. He hated the Christians because they believed in the teachings of Christ and not the law. In his heart he thought he was doing the right thing. Until one day on the road to Damascus he (Paul formerly Saul) encountered Jesus. Along the way, Jesus asked "Saul, Saul why are you persecuting Me?" Acts 22:7 That event was life changing for Paul. Not only did he become a Christian but he was chosen by Christ himself to be an Apostle to the gentiles.

Today people who do not believe in God or the existence of God are called atheist. They refuse to believe God is real. I wonder do they ever ponder the creation of trees, clouds in the sky, the origin of animals, or what causes night and day. Scientist came up with the theory that everything in the universe was a result of a cosmic force they call the Big Bang Theory. Not so! According to God's word, God created everything in the heavens and the earth (Genesis 1)

Even as a child I knew there was a God somewhere. Being taught at an early age to say my prayers, going to church, and having the Bible read to me helped my belief grow. As an adult I got to know God for myself. I travel a lot and I get to see so much of the beauty in God's creations. Proof is all around. I simply cannot understand how they can say there is no God.

Prayer: Father God help those who do not believe in you. Open their understanding of who you truly are that they might fully believe. Open their spiritual eyes that they may see you clearly and take hold of eternal life by obeying the glorious gospel of Jesus Christ. In Jesus Name, Amen.

24 YOUR CROSS

Then Jesus told his disciples," If anyone would come after me, let him deny himself and take up his cross and follow me. Matthew 16:24

In the old days Romans crucified many Christians on the cross. This was a horrific way to die. They were oftentimes beaten first then nailed to the cross. Hanging on the cross for hours before they died. Sometimes it was for a crime they may have committed and sometimes it was just because they believed in Jesus. The worst crucifixion was when they crucified Jesus. He came to the world for that purpose. To help mankind out of their sin problem. They killed our Lord in such a way that He was not even recognizable. The thing is He went to the cross willingly so that you and I would have a chance to live again after death. He took the sting out of death.

What does it mean to you to pick up and carry your cross? To carry your cross is to pay whatever it costs to follow our Lord and Savior Jesus Christ. In times past, as I mentioned earlier, those who followed Jesus were persecuted and hung on the cross. In today's times we must deal with family members, friends and some in our society who don't believe in our Lord.

I can attest to that. Coming in off the streets and allowing God to have his way in my life, many who knew of me and my background thought that it was impossible for me to trade in a life of partying, drugging, and everything that came under that umbrella to give my life to the Lord. They would talk about me, ridicule me and say that it would never last. I felt the heavy burden of carrying my cross at first but then after some time changing my environment and giving that burden to the Lord, my load became a lot easier. Jesus will carry you through. Whatever burdens you may be carrying today give them to Jesus. The word declares "cast all your cares upon him for he careth for you" (1Peter 5:7). The word careth means he continually cares for you. It never ends. That is good news, right? Hang in there and give it all to the Lord. He carried the cross for you and me many years ago.

Prayer: Father God thank you for sending your one and only Son to die on that old, rugged cross for the whole world but especially for a sinner like me. Remind me when I feel the burdens of this world closing all around me that You care and you are here for me. In Jesus name, Amen.

Made in the USA
Columbia, SC
21 March 2022

57757699R00030